Book 1

This book offers the reader the opportunity to read words with the suffixes s, es, ed and ing. It is complemented by the Amber Guardians workbook. The range of activities in the workbook will help the reader to understand the structure of the words and to comprehend and spell them.

Contents

Chapter 1: Trouble at the Market

"Finn!" An excited cry rang out across the noisy hum of the bazaar. "I knew it was you, as soon as I spotted that cloak. I'm sure you've been wearing it since you were thirteen!"

Finn had been browsing the stalls for a gift for his mother. "Izzy!" he said in surprise. A tall girl with blonde spiky hair and a wide grin appeared. He hugged her warmly. "I thought you were still travelling?"

"I was," grinned Izzy, tapping a leather pouch in her pocket. "And we found some fantastic new healing herbs." Izzy was often away with her dad, collecting rare plant samples.

She pointed down at a pair of feet sticking out from under a stall next to them. "We got back late last night. Kit already has me out tracking down climbing hooks!"

A boy with round glasses and a lively face emerged from under the stall beside Izzy.

He was busy inspecting a handful of rusty hooks he had found under the stall.

"Great. I knew I'd find good ones here," he mumbled.

"Finn!" smiled Kit, as he looked up. "It's surprising to see you on dry land! Where's Korus?"

Finn, a fisherman, had met a talking songbird called Korus during an epic adventure at sea.

"Korus? He's flown south for the winter," answered Finn.

Just then a crowd of people began to push past them. "Stop that thief!" bellowed a sudden loud voice. "Grab him! Don't let him get away!"

A tiny barrel of fur shot out of the crowd of bodies and hurled itself into Finn's arms. Finn looked affectionately at the tiny monkey, now clinging to him. He rolled his eyes.

"Monk! What have you been up to now?" Monk thrust a metal chain into Finn's hand. He clung to Finn's chest. His tiny blue eyes were

wide with fear.

"I said grab him!" yelled an angry stall keeper. He pushed his way through the crowd towards them. He pointed angrily at Monk. "He's a thief!" he spat. "You need to pay for what he has stolen!"

"I'm so sorry, sir," apologised Finn. "He's a monkey. He doesn't understand he can't just pick things up if they don't belong to him." He looked at the man respectfully. "Please, whatever it is, let me pay for it, sir," he begged.

Izzy was hiding a smile. "I see Monk is up to his old tricks," she whispered to Kit, as Finn pleaded with the irate stall keeper.

Kit grinned and began searching through his pockets for cash. "Can we pay for it, sir?" he echoed. He held out a handful of battered notes.

They had just enough cash to calm down the angry stall keeper. "Keep him at home next time!" he snarled as he left. "In a cage if you have one!"

Finn had found Monk washed up on a beach, half-starved and with a badly injured leg. Nobody knew Monk's past. Finn had nursed him back to health and the two were now inseparable.

"You are a disaster, Monk," said Finn, with a grin. He rubbed the tiny monkey's chin affectionately.

"What did Monk pick up from that stand?" asked Izzy curiously. "Hopefully something you can give your mum for her birthday!"

Finn pulled the strange-looking necklace out of his pouch.

Chapter 2: A Strange-Looking Necklace

"Wow, it's lovely," gasped Izzy. She reached forward to pick it up. The battered necklace was very old and badly damaged. Most of its original jewels were missing.

"Lovely junk," snorted Kit. "Think how many climbing hooks we could have bought with all that cash. Finn's mum will just throw it away." He glanced at the necklace dismissively. "It only has one jewel left in it."

Izzy gazed at the necklace. A spidery metal clasp held the one large remaining jewel. She rubbed the dust off it with her fingers. It glowed with a soft orange light.

"You're wrong, Kit," she said, her eyes sparkling with excitement. "This looks like real amber!"

Sunlight lit up the amber jewel, picking out the shadows deep inside it. Izzy stared at the beautiful stone. It was odd. It almost looked as if something inside it was moving.

All of a sudden, Finn felt uneasy. Cold prickles of fear made him shudder. He had a strong feeling that they were being observed. From the corner of his eye he saw a figure slipping silently away into the shadows. Had someone been watching them? Were they looking for the necklace? Or was it just his own fear playing tricks on him?

"It's time to move on," he told the others. "I have a feeling there may be more to this necklace than we think."

Izzy hadn't seen the shadowy figure watching them. She was still excited about the necklace. "Do you think it could be lost treasure?" she asked. Her eyes glinted hopefully.

"If it is, then it's been lost for a long time!" laughed Kit. "It looks as if it's been at the bottom of the sea for about a hundred years!"

"I know someone who can value it," said Izzy. "A shopkeeper my dad has talked about."

"Worth a try, I guess," shrugged Kit. He was busy hanging his new climbing hooks onto his belt.

There was no sign now of anyone watching them. Finn began to relax. The necklace was just a broken tangle of metal from a junk stall. No one would be looking for it.

They strolled through the market to the tiny shop Izzy had spoken about. They pushed their way through a heavy velvet curtain. The darkened room was filled with piles of strange twisted metal.

"Now, this IS treasure," breathed Kit as they gazed around them. The room smelled of mouldy paper, damp and decay. A flickering light came from candles, half hidden in piles of dusty junk. Finn blinked as his eyes slowly adjusted to the gloom. An old man stepped through a curtain hidden in the shadows. He peered suspiciously at them through thick reading glasses.

"Can I help you?" he muttered. "What brings you here?" The shopkeeper gasped when he saw the broken necklace Izzy held out to him.

He stepped backwards, away from them, his eyes glued on it fearfully.

"Well, he certainly doesn't look very happy to see us ... or that necklace," whispered Kit.

"It's beautiful," admitted the shopkeeper, "but it comes with the threat of terrible danger. Dark spies will be searching for it. They are servants of the old sorcerer, seeking what was lost."

Chapter 3: Danger in the Shadows

The shopkeeper stopped speaking suddenly, as if he regretted having spoken.

The word 'danger' triggered different responses in the three friends. Kit's eyes lit up and he looked at the necklace with renewed interest. Izzy gazed at it in horror. Finn wanted to find out more.

"Please, will you take a closer look at it, sir?" he begged. He stepped forward towards the retreating shopkeeper. At that moment a hooded figure leapt down from the rafters above them. He crashed into Finn and tried to snatch the necklace from Izzy's shaking fingers.

Kit rushed to help. He pushed hard against a tall bookcase. The heavy books rained down on the dark figure.

"Run!" hissed the shopkeeper. He pressed a scrap of paper into Finn's hand. "Follow the directions to the old town. The answers you seek are in the ruins of the old museum."

He gestured at the hooded figure, slumped on the floor. "Make haste before this dark spy wakes up," he urged. "Please, never return here. This is the last time I will help you. I have carried the weight of a terrible secret for many years. It is your turn now to take it on."

With no time for discussion, they ran from the shop and raced along the streets. Monk clung silently to Finn's shoulder. Izzy knew this part of town well. She led them down a maze of dark alleyways. The other two soon had no idea where they were heading. The three of them looked nervously behind them as they ran. They were terrified of seeing the hooded figure following them.

"He's coming!" gasped Izzy suddenly, in panic. "There, beside those crates. He's looking for us!" They pressed themselves into a darkened doorway, hearts beating crazily.

"It's getting late," panted Kit. "The streets are emptying and he'll be able to see us!" He squinted upwards. "We'll have a better chance if we go across the rooftops!"

Izzy's face revealed her fear even before she spoke. "The rooftops, Kit? Are you joking? Monk might make it, but the rest of us will break our necks!"

Kit knew Izzy was terrified of heights. "Please, Iz," he said gently. "That dark spy isn't someone we want to meet in a hurry and he's about to spot us." He felt along the wall behind him. "This door is open. It's our escape route."

They slid through the door and raced up a flight of steps. Their feet clattered against the stone as they headed for the tiled roof.

"We'll need to jump from one rooftop to another," said Kit. "Treat it as a game," he urged Izzy. "Don't overthink it. Just take it one step at a time."

They raced along the rooftops, jumping from one building to the next. Izzy was white-faced with fear, but she kept up with the others. Years of travelling with her dad had taught her to be fast and nimble, especially in the face of danger.

It was easy at first as the buildings were close together. Suddenly they reached a place where they needed to jump across a huge gap to reach the next building. Izzy's face screwed up in fear.

"You can do it, Iz," urged Kit. "Just don't look down." The three of them leapt bravely towards the next building, but the gap was too wide.

Suddenly they were falling! A chill wind howled past their ears as they dropped rapidly towards the ground. There was no escape!

Finn reached desperately for Izzy's hand. Seconds away from crashing to the ground, their fall was softened by a huge canvas. It was stretched between the two buildings.

Chapter 4: An Amazing Discovery

They lay trembling in the safe hammock of canvas, winded and terrified by their fall. "That was close," gasped Finn.

"You can say that again," said Izzy. "It's too far to jump. Let's find a safe way down."

They peered down into the gloomy space below them.

Kit took the rope from around his waist. He threaded it through a metal hook in the wall beside them. One by one they used the rope to slowly lower themselves down. Finn peered around.

"It looks like we're in the ruins of an old courtyard," he whispered. He gazed up at a dark, ruined building.

"Luckily, we've lost that creepy spy!" added Izzy with relief. Finn nodded, but he couldn't shake off the feeling that something was watching them. The silent building around them felt full of dark secrets. It towered over them, as if waiting for them to make a move. "Let's move on," he urged the others.

"Finn!" gasped Izzy suddenly, pointing at the necklace in Finn's hand. "Look at the amber jewel!"

The jewel had begun to glow with a soft orange light. It started to vibrate. Odd shadows whirled inside it like a miniature tide.

"It's as if it is trying to help us," said Izzy in wonder. Finn held up the necklace.

The space around them slowly began to take shape in the strange orange light.

Kit had a sudden realisation. "This is the courtyard of the ruined museum! We've landed exactly where we need to be!"

Kit led them across the courtyard and into the museum. The building had been in ruins for years. They explored a long corridor of locked wooden doors. Each one was guarded by a broken stone statue. Eventually they arrived at a heavy wooden door that opened into a huge hall.

Pools of coloured light spilled onto the floor from a cracked stained-glass window. Izzy clutched Finn's arm and pointed across the hall. A huge golden map stretched across the dusty wall.

"It's a map of the ancient kingdom," whispered Izzy in amazement. "My father has talked about that place for years. I thought it only existed in his dreams. This must be what we've been sent to find!"

As they gazed at the map, the light from the amber jewel in Finn's hand began to vibrate more brightly. It seemed to be urging them even further onwards. The flickering orange light revealed a huge statue of a warrior holding a mighty sword.

Suddenly, Finn noticed a round purple orb in the warrior's hand. The orb was the size of a large orange. It was made of a totally different material to the rest of the statue. He saw a pulsing light deep inside it.

"We need to get that purple orb," Finn shouted. "There is some connection between it and the amber jewel in the necklace."

Kit wasted no time. He began to clamber up the stone statue, as nimbly as a spider. This was territory he knew well.

Kit clambered along the statue's arm like a panther on a thick tree branch. He began to inch towards the purple orb. It shimmered as he touched it. He tried to prise it loose using his climbing hook. It was no good. The orb was stuck fast in the statue's hand.

Suddenly a blinding light filled the hall. The massive door at the entrance was flung open. A horrifying cyclops appeared in the lit doorway. It glared crazily from one bloodshot eye in the middle of its forehead. It scanned the room.

At its side was the hooded spy! He was controlling the cyclops with a device. It gave out strange blue energy waves.

Under the control of the hooded spy, the cyclops lunged across the room. It began to attack the statue with a massive stone hammer.

The statue began to fracture. Huge shards of heavy grey rock rained to the ground. A sudden terrifying cracking sound filled the air.

The statue's stone arm crumbled and collapsed. Kit was thrown off the statue in an explosion of rubble.

"Kit!" yelled Izzy, in panic. The purple orb tumbled to the ground. Izzy raced to grab it.

Izzy retreated into the shadows as a cloud of dust filled the room.

Finn handed Monk the necklace. "Take it to Izzy," he whispered. "This beast mustn't get the amber jewel, even if it gets me." He weaved crazily across the floor, trying to distract the cyclops away from the others. "Come on, monster. Follow me!" he yelled.

The cyclops struggled to track Finn with its one bleary eye. It swung its hammer wildly, trying to catch Finn.

Kit, winded from his fall, was lying in the dust. He stirred now and staggered to his feet. He threw himself bravely at the hooded spy, knocking him to the floor. The strange controlling device was lost in a sea of rubble.

Without the spy as his controller, the cyclops was filled with confusion. It shook its massive head from side to side. Thick strings of saliva sprayed from its disgusting mouth.

Monk ran to Izzy. He thrust the necklace into her hand. Instinct made her put it around her neck. She had a sudden strong feeling that the purple orb was calling to her. What was she supposed to do?

She ran her fingers over it. It made no sense to her. She noticed something strange. The orb was not complete. It had a deep empty socket at its centre.

The amber jewel and the purple orb in her hand were both now pulsing wildly. Izzy grasped the amber jewel. She twisted it sharply and yanked it off the necklace. She thrust it into the empty socket in the purple orb.

Chapter 6: A Giant Creature

White mist poured from the purple orb. A giant winged creature slowly took shape before them. He flexed his muscular limbs and unfurled huge, powerful wings. The hooded spy retreated in terror and tripped over his feet as he raced for the doorway. The amber jewel dropped back out of the purple orb. Izzy jammed it back into the necklace.

The powerful winged creature had been released from the amber jewel! He reared up defiantly on his massive hind legs.

The puzzled cyclops backed away. It howled one last roar of confusion, then stumbled from the room. Finn felt the hairs on the back of his neck prickle with fear. Was this creature a friend or an enemy? He stepped forward bravely to face him.

The creature's flecked eyes softened. He spoke in a deep rumbling tone.

"The three of you have released me. I need to ask for your help, but I know it will place you in great danger."

Kit grinned. "We're in! Tell us what to do!"

"Should we?" Finn asked Izzy softly.

Joy and relief surged through Izzy. By some miracle they had escaped both a cyclops and a dark spy. Now they were being offered an adventure.

"You and Kit are my best friends. If you're in, then I'm in," she said with a grin.

The creature lowered his head towards them. "I am humbled by your trust. An evil sorcerer from the past has resurfaced. Our world is no longer safe. I am one of ten powerful Guardians," he told them. "You released me when you put the amber jewel into the orb in your hand. My nine friends are still trapped in amber jewels scattered across the ancient kingdom. Together, the ten of us can destroy the sorcerer and his dark forces."

He paused, his voice softening. "Will you come with me to the ancient kingdom and release the other Guardians?"

He stretched out his massive wings. "There is no time to lose. Take your places on my back and we can begin our quest ... "

Glossary

affectionately	– lovingly, tenderly
amber	– a yellow or brown fossil resin often made into jewellery
bleary	– blurred or dimmed
browsing	– casually looking through things for sale
clamber	– climb using hands and feet
clattered	– made a loud, rattling noise
emerged	– moved away from something and became visible
flexed	– tightened
fracture	– break or split
glinting	– giving out tiny, quick flashes of light
haste	– hurry
inseparable	– can't be parted
instinct	– a natural impulse, not thought through

irate	– very angry
nimble	– quick and light in movement
pulsing	– throbbing
resurfaced	– came to the surface again
shimmered	– shone with a faint light
shudder	– tremble with fear or cold
socket	– a hollow part of something, designed for something else to fit into
squinted	– looked with his eyes partly closed
thrust	– shoved
unfurled	– opened out from a folded state
urged	– persuaded